Memorable Daze

Zemaye Okediji

BookLeaf
Publishing

Presentation by *BookLeaf Publishing*

Web: www.bookleafpub.com

E-mail: info@bookleafpub.com

ISBN: 9789395950749

First edition 2022

This is dedicated to my mum, Grace Z. Egbagbe and my brother, Nkemka Ekwueme.

ACKNOWLEDGEMENT

I'd like to acknowledge the following people who played a role in developing some of the noteworthy moments that inspired this collection of poems: my family and friends Maureen Osuji and Ayoola Williams.

Special thanks to Lisa Pascal, Gwen Short, Charlotte Boston, Halima Abubakar-Idrisu, Oguike Nwaneri and Oge, Audrey Simmons, Jenni Schaefer and to my colleagues at CREATE Art Center and my peers at Heart and Soul DMV.

PREFACE

I am a mental health care advocate who believes in the efficacy of the creative process and the power of expression to support overall well-being. I wrote Memorable Daze to demonstrate that adopting a creative routine can have positive outcomes especially after you work through a challenging creative process.

This collection of poems will resonate with anyone who likes to make meaning out of words and develop imagery to compliment prose.

This archive of sorts, invites you on a 21-day journey into my world characterized by celebrations, apprehensions and conversations that challenge you to develop your own interpretation of the life events and characters and to unlock any private messages they may hold.

Memorable Daze is a response to the write angle challenge and my attempt to produce my first publication – a body of work that embodies the intersection of imagery, rhythm and therapy as my artistic contribution to the world.

Neuve Nueve

One day
D-Day
Berth day
Two ways
One birth, another berth
Travail and soul sail
Awed rays
Relax vanes
Celebrate flight, release light
Shine ever-bright
Today today
Accentuate life
'Cos that One day is Today

Yes, I do VM

Perfect day pray tell
For a birthday très belle
Marry me in stead

Up goes my flute, CLUNK!
Edison lights video
Shock wipes out sunset

Olamide

25 topical conditions like ingrown hairs
I hate to say, I dabble GIRL
Connection is fuzzy
Connection is futile
Connection is mental
Health is worthwhile
$5 million Deja Vu, I see you--beautiful
Beauty that's skin deep
Inspiring connections so steep
Material to people
For 25 topical conditions
Making connections beautiful
And connections futile
But for connections for people to themselves

Gratia

She was winded
She was wounded
She was waiting
In glorious patience
The original supernova
1st generation star power
To hear her winded
Was a snare to my eardrum
Something to hate
Even though it was bliss
For a chance to rest
And delicately find comfort in frailty
Because above all else, I put the lover of my soul first
Accepting the extended privilege
Of love & connective tissue & effervescent blood lines
That serve plebeian pie
With peaches and kola nut
As a white flag offering to the truth
That the honorable lover of my soul, loved her too
...and still will do

Me & the D

Here, there, nowhere and everywhere
An echo of ethical orders
Unsure if it's worth the bother
Study faux pas'
From Charlotte to Boston
And recovered Gwendionnas
Down more water, chug more pasta
Embrace the skinny against the Anal-rexia
And model that therapeutic wear
Surely labor today bears no tot,
What-the-fuuuuu...
Want what Tree? How'd you Feel?
About the DDs!

Testosterone

Pitter Patter
Pitter Patter
The universe's spittle splatters
Tributaries to begin the ride
At Private Ryan's reflective glimpse

Splish Splash
Splish Splash
Goes the circulator zooming past
Way past 13th and almost through nine
But for non-ambiguous grey mama
Calling out that bebestic driver

Swish Swoosh
Swish Swoosh
Came the shuffle of every object
Of this mind-splitting concert
Flagging this and flagging that
Helping the orchestra, timing out

Dry palms, frazzled members
Bode "It's brutal!" to all examiners
A moment of shock, a pause, a stare
And we picked up our feelings going absolutely nowhere

Tick Tock
Tick Tock
Give me a taco
Show me a truck
Dish that baklava
Now we are down on luck

Ring Ring
Ring Ring
Show me a couple
Of lovely soles
Shining bright smiles
Sounds in all caps

Tick Tock
Tick Tock
Hair love, beep bops
Peep show, Oh no! no! no!
Breathless Alpha
Hysterical Beta
Sprung Delta

Praying this, praying that
Malfunctioning will not last
An emergent scene

Swish Swoosh
Swish Swoosh

Creaking fantasy of stretcher in place of the chair
She's the oxygen and flooding creek here

Splish Splash
Splish Splash
Nebulous dilated eyes
Doctored emergent scene synergized
With visions of exchanged contacts
And deluded valiance
"Oh He-da-man!" You-Elle!

Pitter Patter
Pitter Patter
Heavy is the heart that bears the matter
Of bringing the star to the show
For that same reflective glimpse, now a glow
That is, saving private ryan

Art Therapy I

Beckoning

Aplomb consciousness

Leverage all resources

A pilgrimage of aches and pains, inn-to-inn
explore

Nefarious character of cozy, comfy, warm, and
Rocky vigor

Contemplate misguided perception and process

Expeditions of traipsed tour punctuating the
fulcrum more

Blind G Spot

Feelings I could not feel
Made it so that nothing was real
The rejections and violations that never took place and so couldn't ever heal
In a distant past now a recessed memory
I had no words for this energy
I paused and pondered until it became clear to me that this spell cost me dearly
Reactive emotions that my eyes could not see were disguised to be
The very embodiment of perfection and character flaw that ensured my blind spot held me oblivious to those feelings
All in a moment, oh-so-real

V.O.N.

White pearls shattering through shadows and
doubt
Of textbook chemistry
The cool calm collectedness recovers from every
test tube fallout
This test tube of pearls go together like 5 & 6
Rhythm and blues, the boo of a ghost that's you
Into the sunset with soft celestial elegance
The onyx irradiated circles exhibiting its
apparent fervor --
Naturally, they became o' stars

LimLim

How do you box a shadow mind?
Do you mark it?
group it?
express it?
lose it?
And how do you know when you don't use it?

"Mind your language," he schooled
"Hidden identity," she understood
Interpreted as protective, medicinal and potentially therapeutic
Her true identity was politics shy, IDP uninterested yet empathetic
An intentional shadow mind, out of frame yet in focus
For the highest honor yet -- a reality named artist

Too Much Sam

Drip drench envelope
Brand new staccato stoke
Seeping tenderness

Pascal

Months in lines, shape and form
A picture offering how we perform
On busy days, our hectic ways
A reflection of reality at every stage
Mentholatum and hospitalization
Reminders that we are out of our jurisdiction
Months in lines, shape our form
With colors that express time twisted without
succor

JenniEd

Ed has such range she told
Slow to manifest and hard to detect spread that showed
Never to shy away from getting fed
I got JenniEd with a salmon plate instead

Humptea Dumpday

Tremors of terror
Post op derriere cannon
Sac full of fluid
Photo op candid
Canal steering generations
To unbridled genius
Tremors of terror
Galvanized by some foreign fervor

Kelz and locs

Kelt
Energy
Ladened
Zeal
Butterfly lockets released SOC appeal

FFFFidels

The romeo to her jolié ate
An almond pretzel, a churro twisted hotdog taco
Craving a chicha morada
Two Proseccos, the boujier order
In celebration of the silver lining
Polkadot orange spring chicas to a high end

Create a-way

Lemon splice
Sweet tart
Bleeding heart
Artsy fart
Breezeway through a hearty broadcast

Amethyst

Camillus
Golden hour
Heartfelt au pair
The woman king resonates
Honor

Vegan

Broken strides
Heavy tides
Luscious cake
Camaraderie makes
Green hair
Barely there
Motherly vibes
Weatherproof chide
Nostalgic confide
Reclaimed tide
Divinely swept
A peppy step
To a transformed stride

1:00 Musings

11th hour, no 1st
A tinkle a tattle
With thoughts of subliminal psychobabble
A birthday or two or three
Cake and company of drunken remind
When of 7, three decline
Beckoning the thought "Oh I really shouldn't have"
Of weekend sojourns

A beginning that feels like an end
As subcon memories of a ring-ish road entale
Vier left against a hilly ascent right
With the softest, gentlest prettiest kin
In rattiwear except of silk
Woven to perfection and luxurious for conversation
"Oh boy, why you go this way?" was the only question
"I want you to see my house" felt like a cover-up mention
How time had flown by and this was just a compound
Lugbe it was, Samson it showed, Peter echoed
Wherever were we now?

In our subcon version of GOT?
Surely Ay-bee-jay over Eh-doe
Or gbomo gbomo express with an impending
tailspin

Ayoola

The promise was revealed
Accord never ceased
The dream suffered draconian trials
Under no shut-eye contact Jacobian rivals
Protection was never sealed
For you, em...promise that was revealed

www.ingramcontent.com/pod-product-compliance
Lightning Source LLC
Chambersburg PA
CBHW051754130826
49812CB00033B/1150